IN MEMORY OF JOHNATHON

© 2024 by Amy Parker
All Rights Reserved

Published in 2024 by
Walking Together Press
Estes Park, Colorado USA
Jenta Mangoro, Jos, Plateau Nigeria
walkingtogether.press

ISBN: 978-1-961568-74-7

Unless otherwise noted, all Scripture quotations are taken from the Holman Christian Standard Bible®, Copyright © 1999, 2000, 2002, 2003, 2009 by Holman Bible Publishers. Used by permission. Holman Christian Standard Bible®, Holman CSB®, and HCSB® are federally registered trademarks of Holman Bible Publishers.

Scripture quotations marked NASB are taken from the New American Standard Bible®, Copyright © 1960, 1962, 1963, 1968, 1971, 1972, 1973, 1975, 1977, 1995 by the Lockman Foundation. Used by permission. (www.lockman.org).

Scripture quotations noted as NCV are taken from the New Century Version®. Copyright © 2005 by Thomas Nelson. Used by permission. All rights reserved. Scripture quotations marked NIV are taken from the Holy Bible, NEW INTERNATIONAL VERSION®. Copyright © 1973, 1978, 1984 by Biblica, Inc. All rights reserved worldwide. Used by permission.

Book and cover design by: Jacoba Looije

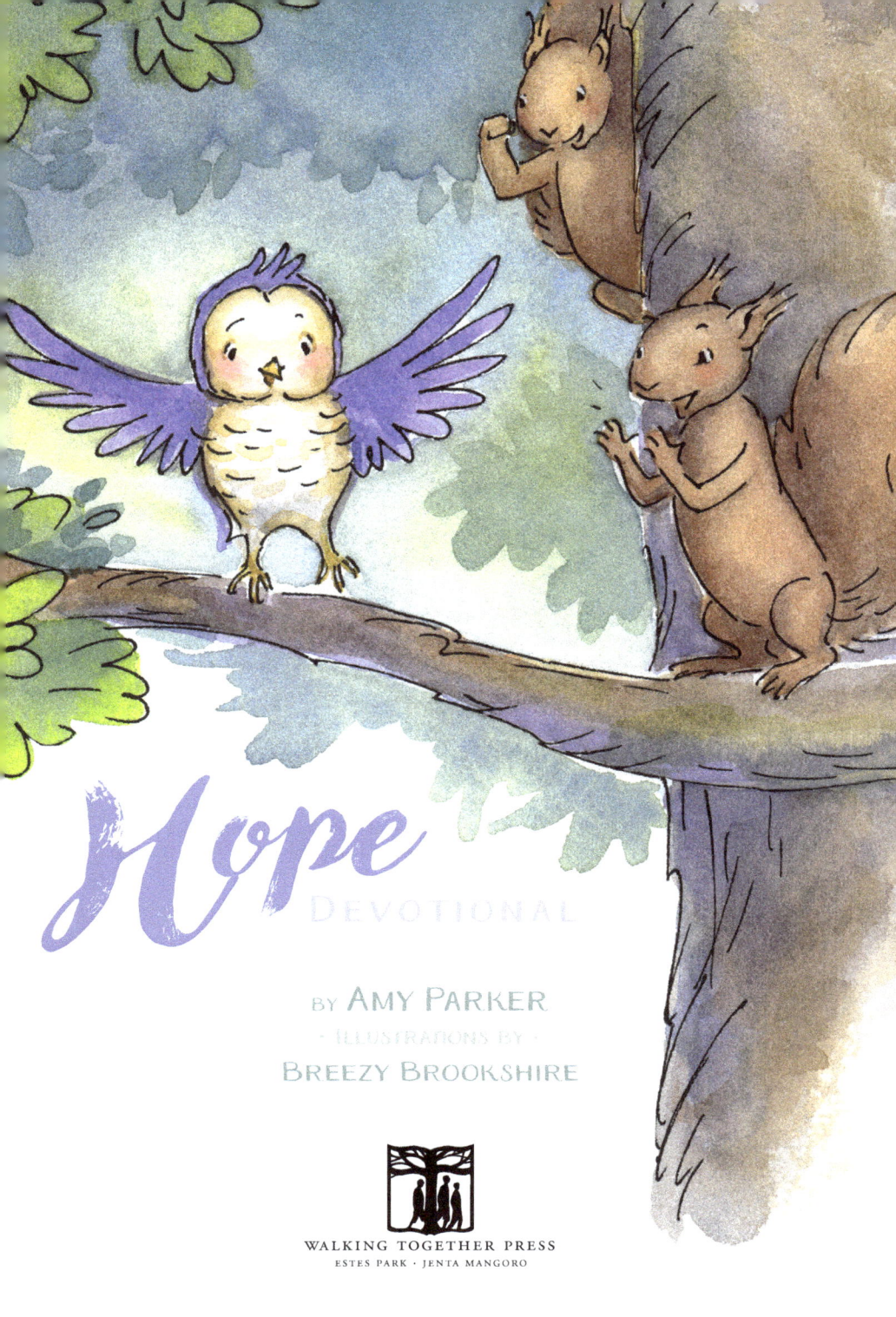

Hope
DEVOTIONAL

BY AMY PARKER
ILLUSTRATIONS BY
BREEZY BROOKSHIRE

WALKING TOGETHER PRESS
ESTES PARK · JENTA MANGORO

Contents

Have Hope 2
The Hope Factory 4
Strength and Courage 6
Faithful Love 8
He Will Answer 10
What Are You Waiting For? 12
The Cure for Sadness 14
What He Has Done 16
Awe-Inspiring Works 18
False Hope 20
Rest in Him 22
My Hope, My Confidence 24
Day and Night 26
God's Promises = Hope 28
What Hope? 30
Disappearing Hope 32
Hope in Justice 34
Hope in Waiting 36

God's Chosen People	38
Hope in Your Helper	40
Valuable You	42
Choose Wisely	44
Hope = Joy	46
Stay Hopeful	48
You CAN	50
Hope in Wisdom	52
Finding Strength	54
A Future and a Hope	56
Never-Ending Love	58
Get Rid of the Worries	60
The Hope of the World	62
Hope Grows	64
Always Hope	66

Hope DEVOTIONAL

Have Hope

You should have confidence because you respect God; you should have hope because you are innocent.

—Job 4:6 NVC

Have you heard the story of Job? If so, you may be thinking it has little to do with *hope*. Even though God Himself described Job as "an honest and innocent man" (Job 1:1 ncv), Job lost everything: his children, his wealth, and his health.

Pretty hopeless, huh?

But when you look closer, you see the word *hope* all over the book of Job—eighteen times, in fact—more than almost every other book of the Bible. Job's story is the ultimate test of hope, and he passed with flying colors. No matter what Satan threw at him, Job refused to blame God. Even though Job didn't understand why it was happening, his hope in God remained.

In the end, God gave Job ten more children and *doubled* the riches he had lost. God rewarded Job for having hope in Him. And He will do the same for you.

 **Tell me about it**
Describe a time that felt hopeless to you.

Think about it
How did it turn out? Was it really, truly "hopeless"?

 **DO IT!**
Read the last chapter of Job's story, Job 42, and know that God wants to be your source of hope too.

The Hope Factory

Patience produces character, and character produces hope.

—Romans 5:4 NCV

What if we could have our own little hope factory? You know, a way to produce hope whenever we need it, creating it in an endless supply.

Well, Romans 5:4 tells us exactly how to do that.

First, you take a little patience. Or maybe a whole lot of patience—depending on how much hope you want to make. You patiently wait for God's answers. You patiently watch for His plans. You patiently listen for His will. And before you know it, a little *character* rolls off the factory line.

Then you mold that character into shape. You make good decisions. You think better thoughts. You have better behavior. And that's when you start to see your final product: hope.

The more you work at this process, the more you know this process works. And that produces hope for better things. So, when you get discouraged, just keep piling on the patience; then character will grow and rise into hope.

Tell me about it
Are you needing a little extra hope? Why?

Think about it
What could you do if you had an endless supply of hope?

DO IT!
On a piece of paper, draw your hope factory.

Strength and Courage

Be strong and courageous, all you who put your hope in the Lord.

—Psalm 31:24

What are you afraid of? Thunderstorms? Math tests? The big dog next door?

Well, you don't have to be afraid. There may be a lot of scary things in this world, but God is bigger than all those things. And when you put your hope and faith and trust in Him, He becomes a part of you. He lives inside you. And "the One who is in you is greater than the one who is in the world" (1 John 4:4).

When you put your hope in God, you become braver. You become stronger. And everything else becomes a lot less scary.

Tell me about it
What are you afraid of?

Think about it
How does God, the Creator of the universe, compare to those things?

DO IT!
Talk to God for a minute. Tell Him that you put your hope in Him, and ask Him to give you the strength and courage to face the things that scare you.

Faithful Love

May Your faithful love rest on us, Yahweh, for we put our hope in You.

—Psalm 33:22

What do you put your hope in? Who do you trust with your future? What do you depend on to make your dreams come true? Your parents? Your friends? Your toys? Your home?

All of those are good things, but there's one place we can put our hope that will never let us down. And that is *in the* Lord.

Our parents can't always be there to guide us. Our friends, our toys, even our homes will come and go. But God lasts forever. He knows and sees everything. You can't even imagine His love for you, and His love lasts forever (Psalm 136:1).

Put your hope in the Lord, and His "faithful love" will never let you down.

Tell me about it
Tell about a time when someone let you down.

💡 Think about it
Can you remember a time when you let someone else down?

 DO IT!
Make sure you forgive the person who let you down, and ask forgiveness (if you haven't already) for letting someone else down. And remember to put your hope in God, who will never let us down.

When you read today's verse, what do you think? Do you *really* believe it's true?

When you pray, when you tell God your worries, when you ask for God's help, do you really expect Him to answer?

He *will*, you know. You may not hear it, and it may not be right away. But over time, you will see it. You will feel it.

So as you pray today, say it like you mean it. Say it like God is listening. Say it as if He will answer you.

Because *He will*.

Tell me about it
What prayers has God answered for you?

💡 Think about it
What is a prayer that God hasn't answered? Why do you think that is?

✋ DO IT!
Get a small notebook or a piece of paper. Start a list of prayers that God has answered. As that list grows, your hope in the Lord will grow too.

What Are You Waiting For?

Now, Lord, what do I wait for? My hope is in You.

—Psalm 39:7

Now that your hope is in the Lord ... Now that your strength comes from Him ... Now that you have nothing to fear ...

What are you waiting for?!

What is that big, crazy dream? Or that tiny thing you wanted to change? Or that person you want to become friends with?

You can do it! All of it! Your hopes, your dreams, are waiting! Your fears and worries are gone!

Only hope in Him, and take the next step.

Come on! What are you waiting for?

 Tell me about it
What's one thing you've always wanted to do?

 **Think about it**
Why haven't you done it?

DO IT!
Today, think of that one thing you want to do, something you know God is guiding you to do, and DO IT.

The Cure for Sadness

Why am I so sad? Why am I so upset? I should put my hope in God and keep praising him.

—Psalm 42:5 NCV

There are a lot of sad things that can happen in life. Friends may move away. You may get sick or hurt. You may lose a pet or a loved one.

We can't know for sure why sad things happen to us. They may help us learn and grow. They can help us enjoy the happy times even more.

But there's one thing we know for sure: even when bad things happen, when we feel sad and out of control, God still loves us. And He is still in control.

So when sad days come, as hard as it may seem, remember to put your hope in God, and "keep praising Him."

Tell me about it
When is the last time you were really sad?

Think about it
Did you know that, even then, God was watching over you, loving you?

DO IT!
On a piece of paper, write Psalm 42:5 in bright, colorful letters. Then the next time you're sad, remember to put your hope in God.

Have you ever been told to "count your blessings"? Have you ever done it? Do you know what it means?

Counting your blessings is simply remembering, listing, *counting* all of the wonderful things God has done for you. When we do, as Psalm 52:9 tells us, we remember to praise God for those things. We remember why we put our hope in Him.

So when your hope is weak, when it seems like there's little to hope for, take a look back at all the things He has done in your life. Count your blessings. Thank Him. And remember that there's a whole list of good reasons why you put your hope in Him.

Tell me about it
Does your hope get weak? When?

💡 Think about it
How can counting your blessings help make your hope stronger?

 DO IT!
Let's do it now: count your blessings. Make a list of all the ways God has blessed you. And when your hope starts to dim, get out your list and count them again.

Awe-Inspiring Works

You answer us in righteousness, with awe-inspiring works, God of our salvation, the hope of all the ends of the earth and of the distant seas.

—Psalm 65:5

Take a moment—right now—to look at the world around you. You won't have to look very far to find something awesome.

The flowers of spring. The sunset on the horizon. The fiery colors of fall. The stars in the sky. God personally crafted, handmade, built from scratch every single one of these awe-inspiring things— and so much more.

This is the God who created you. This is the God watching over you. This is the God you can put your hope in.

Always remember that the God of these "awe-inspiring works" is the very God who holds your hand.

 **Tell me about it**

What do you think is the most awesome thing God created?

💡 **Think about it**

Imagine being there as God created that one thing. Listen to Him speak. See it taking shape. How awesome is our God!

✋ **DO IT!**

Draw a picture of one of God's awe-inspiring works. Share it with someone you love.

You wouldn't go rock climbing with a paper chain for a rope. You wouldn't explore a cave with a candle for a light. And you wouldn't go camping with a box for a tent. Well . . . I guess you *could*, but it probably wouldn't end well.

It's just the same with life. You have to be very careful where you place your hope. When you place your hope in the wrong places, it only sets you up to be disappointed or even hurt.

When you go rock climbing, you choose the strongest rope. When you explore a cave, you shine a flashlight that won't burn out. When you go camping, you sleep in a weatherproof tent.

And when you need someone to lean on *for life*, you don't pick a false hope. You put your hope in God.

Tell me about it
Where are some places where you place your hope?

Think about it
How have those things supported you?
How have they let you down?

DO IT!
Make a list of everything you'd need for our survival kit for life.

Rest in Him

Rest in God alone, my soul, for my hope comes from Him.

—Psalm 62:5

Think about your snuggliest blanket, your softest pillow, the coziest spot in the house. Imagine you're in that spot, lying on the pillow, wrapped in that blanket. Maybe even a plate of warm chocolate chip cookies is waiting nearby. Rest doesn't get any better than that, does it?

Yes. Yes, it does.

Not only can you have your blanket, your pillow, your cozy spot—and even your cookies!—you can rest in God, the Creator of the entire universe.

There is nothing you will face that He cannot handle. Just place all of your worries, your fears, your hopes, and your dreams in His hands. And rest in Him.

 Tell me about it
Where's your favorite place to snuggle up for a nap?

💡 Think about it
What does it mean to rest in God?

✋ DO IT!
Draw a great big hand on a piece of paper. Then write any worries, fears, hopes, and dreams on that hand. Imagine yourself giving all of it to God for Him to take care of. Now rest in Him.

My Hope, My Confidence

For You are my hope, Lord God, my confidence from my youth.

—Psalm 71:5

24

Do you ever wonder . . . *Am I good enough for the team? Am I smart enough to keep up? Why would she want to be my friend?*

Well, stop wondering. Stop worrying. And put your confidence in God. He answers with . . . "You are my child" (1 John 3:1). "You are my creation" (Ephesians 2:10). "And you are wonderfully made" (Psalm 139:14).

Whenever you begin to doubt yourself, remember what God says about you. Let your confidence be *in Him.*

 **Tell me about it**
When do you doubt yourself?

 Think about it
What would God say about your doubts?

 DO IT!
Make a list of the doubts you've had about yourself. Now, beside each doubt, write what God says about you.

Day and Night

I rise before dawn and cry out for help; I put my hope in Your word. I am awake through each watch of the night to meditate on Your promise.

—Psalm 119:147-148

When do you talk to God? In the mornings? At bedtime? Before meals?

Our hope will grow stronger with every moment that we think about or "meditate on" God and His promises. And we will learn more about God and those promises every time we read His Word.

Reading devotionals (like this one!) is a great start. But are there other ways you could be spending more time with Him? Starting each day with a prayer? Reading your Bible every night?

God will reward every moment—day and night—that you spend talking to Him, thinking about Him, and learning about Him and His Word. Not only will you grow closer to the One who knows you best; you will gain hope through His promises for you.

 **Tell me about it**

How often do you spend time with God?

💡 **Think about it**

Could you spend more time with God? How would that help you?

 **DO IT!**

Make a simple schedule of the time you want to spend with God.

The Bible is full of God's promises to His people. You can see His promise to Noah—and to us—with a vibrant rainbow resting in the clouds. You can hear His promise to make Abraham's family have as many people as the stars in the sky—and see it unfold before your very eyes. You'll hear God promise to rescue His people from a mean pharaoh—and watch the Israelites march to safety through the middle of the Red Sea. And best of all, you'll read of His promises to send a Savior to the world—and then hear the angels rejoice as that baby, God's Son, is born to us in Bethlehem.

These promises were written just for us, to give us hope, to remind us of God's great love for His people—for you and for me. Take time to read those promises, because when all else fails, God's promises will always be true.

 Tell me about it

Why do you think God wants us to hear about promises that came true so long ago?

Think about it

What do you think these promises mean for you?

 DO IT!

Take some time now to read about one of God's promises in the Bible. Draw a picture or write in your own words what that promise means to you.

We're so lucky, you and I.

We have people who love us, who want us to know about God. We have people who take the time to tell us about God's promises to us. We have people around us who have been filled with the hope that only God gives, and it overflows to you and to me.

But what about the people around us? Are we overflowing with the hope of God and letting them know where to find it too?

There are people out there who have never heard about God. They've never heard a whisper of the name of Jesus, never held a Bible in their hands.

Do you know anyone like that? Do your friends have the hope of God in their hearts? Does your cousin know that Jesus loves him? Find out! And when you do, let the hope in your heart overflow to them too.

 Tell me about it
Name some people who share the hope of God with you.

💡 Think about it
Who do you know who needs to hear about the love of Jesus?

✋ DO IT!
Draw a picture or write a special scripture, and give it to that person today.

Disappearing Hope

For many days neither sun nor stars appeared, and the severe storm kept raging. Finally all hope that we would be saved was disappearing.

—Acts 27:20

In the book of Acts, we read about Paul on a ship, sailing straight for trouble. He had warned the captain about the stormy seas ahead, but the captain ignored him, determined to reach an island where they would spend the winter.

Then the storm came. It drove the boat out into the ocean, beating it with rain and battering it with wind. The men threw out much of their cargo to lighten their load, but still the wooden boat creaked and crashed in the waves. Hope was disappearing fast.

But Paul's hope was in God. An angel had already told him that he and everyone aboard the ship would be safe, so Paul shared that hope with the others—all 275 of them. Before long, the people were shipwrecked, and the boat was splintered, but God's promise stood true. Not one life was lost. The stranded sailors swam to the nearest island, where they were welcomed and cared for by the people who lived there.

As the boat crumbled beneath Paul's feet, he held tight to the promises of God. And God's promises shone brightly, even through the darkest storm.

📢 Tell me about it
Have you ever felt your hope disappear?

💡 Think about it
What happened? What did you do?

✋ DO IT!
Draw a picture of Paul's ship in the storm.
Show the light of God's hope shining through.

Hope in Justice

I hope in Your judgments.
—Psalm 119:43

Judgment may not seem like something you'd place your hope in, but let's think about it for a minute. What if there were none?

Sure, you'd love for Mom to just forget about that cookie you snuck before dinner. But what if that were true for everyone? What if no one ever received judgment? What if people were never punished when they did something wrong? Can you imagine what the world would be like?

So even though "judgment" isn't always fun, it is another reason we can put our hope in God. He sees every person and everything they do, right or wrong. And He uses His godly wisdom to reward the good and to set the wrongs right.

📢 Tell me about it
Why do we have rules?

💡 Think about it
Why do we get punished when we break those rules?

✋ DO IT!
Make a list of five rules in your home. What does it look like when everyone follows those rules? What would it be like if everyone broke all of those rules?

Hope in Waiting

I wait for Yahweh; I wait and put my hope in His word.

—Psalm 130:5

I remember waiting, as a child, for my daddy to get home from work. Every afternoon at four thirty, his old blue truck would rumble into the driveway, and I would burst out the front door and jump into his arms.

Every day I waited for my daddy. And every day I put my hope in his coming home. Even though I *knew* he was coming home, and I even knew what time, I still watched and waited with hope.

Let's watch and wait for the Lord in the same way. We can place our hopes in knowing that He's there, thinking about us and loving us. And we can watch and wait joyfully, with eyes wide open, just to see when He's going to show up next.

📢 Tell me about it
Can you remember a time when you felt loved by God?

💡 Think about it
How do you know that God is there, watching over you?

✋ DO IT!
Imagine God actually holding you in His arms. How would that feel? What would that look like? Draw a picture or write about it as you imagine it.

God's Chosen People

Israel, put your hope in the Lord, both now and forever.

—Psalm 131:3

Israel was God's chosen people. In the Old Testament, we hear a lot about the Israelites, how they started with just one man and a promise from God. We see how they escaped from Egypt and an evil pharaoh. We watch God give them food and water in the wilderness and lead them into their promised land. Even after all the times that God provided for them and brought them to safety, Psalm 131:3 still reminds those people to put their hope in the Lord, "both now and forever."

See, that message wasn't just for God's chosen people thousands of years ago. That message is for God's chosen people of today and tomorrow. You and me. And generations to come.

Sometimes, even as God's people, even after all that He does to help us out, we need to be reminded where to look when we need hope. And that's okay. But we can know that without a doubt, He'll always be there helping us and guiding us, "both now and forever."

 Tell me about it
Where do you think you'll be in five years? In fifty years?

 Think about it
Where will God be in five years? In fifty years?

 DO IT!
Draw a picture of yourself in fifty years. What will you look like? What will you be doing?

Hope in Your Helper

Happy is the one whose help is the God of Jacob, whose hope is in the Lord his God.

—Psalm 146:5

When you're little, it seems you're always asking for help—with tying your shoes, reaching the cereal, doing your math. And sometimes you just can't wait until you're big enough to do it all on your own!

But do you want to know a secret from a grown-up? Even when you get big and *you're* the parent—tying shoes and reaching cereal and explaining math—you will *still* need help. Paying the bills and raising the kids and doing your job.

Lucky for us, big or little, parent or child, our Helper is always there. He may send His help in the form of a parent or a teacher or a good friend. But if we take our needs to Him, He will be faithful to help us. And as the psalmist reminds us, we are happy when our help and our hope comes from God.

You'll never get so big that you don't need the help of God.

📢 Tell me about it
What are some things you still need help with?

💡 Think about it
What are some things you are now big enough to do on your own?

✋ DO IT!
Talk to God about the things you need help with. And be happy that your help comes from Him.

Valuable You

The Lord values those who fear Him, those who put their hope in His faithful love.

—Psalm 147:11

Has anyone ever told you how much you're worth . . . how much God loves you and values you?

It can be hard to understand that the Creator of the entire universe, who made millions and billions of people, cares about little ol' you. But He does—it's true!

Luke 12:7 says that even "the hairs of your head are all counted." I would dare to guess that your parents don't even know how many hairs are on your head! But that's how much God knows about you, how much He cares about you.

The Creator of the universe has spoken: You are valued. You are loved. You are His.

📣 Tell me about it

Why do you think you're important to God?

💡 Think about it

What are some ways God shows us how much He values us?

✋ DO IT!

Go ahead. Just try to count the number of hairs on your head. Then thank God for loving you so much that He already knows.

Sometimes life just doesn't seem fair. Sometimes it can seem like doing the right thing gets you nowhere. And sometimes it seems like the ones making trouble are the only ones having fun.

This isn't a new thing. It doesn't surprise God. And it shouldn't surprise us.

Thousands of years ago, when the wisest men were putting together the book of Proverbs, they wrote today's verse for you. God knew that one day you would have to make a choice.

When all of your friends are laughing at the new girl . . . When the mess in your room can all be hidden under the bed . . . When your brother is feeding his peas to the dog . . . Choose wisely. "For then you will have a future, and your hope will never fade."

Tell me about it

Have you ever seen someone do something wrong and get away with it? What happened?

Think about it

Why should you choose the right thing, even if no one will know?

DO IT!

Talk to God about making right choices. Ask Him to give you strength to follow in His ways.

Hope = Joy

The hope of the righteous is joy.
—Proverbs 10:28

Imagine a big pile of presents. Tall ones, skinny ones, great big boxy ones. Red stripes, yellow polka dots, and purple curly bows.

You immediately start thinking of all the things that could be inside. And you feel excited . . . happy . . . *hopeful.*

God has a big pile of surprises just waiting for your life. He's wrapping up things you've never even thought of. And by seeking His will and walking in His ways, you can hope, you can know, that one by one, you will unwrap those gifts for your life.

Expect great things from God, and that hope will bring you joy all the days of your life.

Tell me about it
What gifts has God already given you in your life?

Think about it
What kinds of gifts do you think He has waiting for you?

DO IT!
Draw a picture of God's gifts. Include some of the gifts He's given you and some of the gifts you have yet to unwrap.

Stay Hopeful

*Delayed hope makes the heart sick,
but fulfilled desire is a tree of life.*

—Proverbs 13:12

Staying hopeful can be hard! Worry will whine in your ear. Fear will creep into your mind. Waiting will seem to last forever.

But when fear and worry and waiting darken your day, remember to look for the ray of light shining through. That light is your hope, your reminder that God is in control and that He's working for your good.

Tell your fears that God controls them. Tell your worries that He will take care of you. And tell yourself that you can wait one more day (and another and another if you have to). When we choose to focus on the light, it can chase away the darkness every time.

 **Tell me about it**

How do worry and fear affect our hopes?

 **Think about it**

How do our hopes affect our worries and fears?

 **DO IT!**

Get a flashlight and—carefully—go into a dark room. Turn on the flashlight and watch the light chase the darkness away.

You CAN

"Those who put their hope in Me will not be put to shame."

—Isaiah 49:23

You are going to fail at some things in life.

There. I said it. And that's okay. Failing means that you tried. Failing will teach you what *not* to do. And failing will eventually teach you to do some things really, really well.

But whether you're winning or losing, there is no shame when your hope is in the Lord.

Philippians 4:13 reminds us, "I am able to do all things through Him who strengthens me." God will give us the strength to follow His path. And He will give us the strength to get back up when we fail. As long as our eyes are on Him and His grace, the world's idea of failure won't mean a thing.

Put your hope in Jesus. Trust Him. Follow Him. And you will be able to do anything He calls you to do.

📣 Tell me about it
Describe a time when you failed at something.

💡 Think about it
What did you learn from that failure?

✋ DO IT!
Write the words of Philippians 4:13 on a piece of paper. Use bright colors, decorate it with a fun border, and hang it where you and your family can see it.

Hope in Wisdom

"If you find [wisdom], you will have a future, and your hope will never fade.

—Proverbs 24:14

Where is wisdom? Where would you look? Is it up in the sky? Or in a big book?

God gives us so many ways to learn about Him, to gain wisdom about our lives. Of course, the Bible, His Word, is the most complete source of wisdom He's given to us. But He has also surrounded us with people who love us and want to teach us about Him. Our parents and teachers and pastors can help us understand Bible stories and big words like *salvation* and *redemption*. Even just a walk outside, looking at a leaf or a feather or an ant, can tell you so much about this amazing world and the Creator who made it for you.

Be on the lookout for wisdom, wherever you go, and you will be sure to find it. And when you do, "you will have a future, and your hope will never fade."

 **Tell me about it**
Where do you go to learn more about God?

 Think about it
What is one thing you've always wanted to know about God?

 DO IT!
Open your Bible or go to a parent or teacher and start looking for answers about that one thing.

Finding Strength

"You were tired out by the length of your road, yet you did not say, 'It is hopeless.' You found renewed strength, therefore you did not faint."

—Isaiah 57:10 NASB

Imagine this: You're out shopping with Mom. It seems like you've walked down every single aisle of the store at least three times. Your little feet have to do double-time to keep up with her big steps. Your legs are Jell-O.

Do you . . .

    a) whine and complain, and scream, "It is hopeless!"?

    b) smile and find the strength to keep on going?

Read Isaiah 57:10 one more time. I think you know the answer. When life wears you down, look up and smile. You will find new strength in hope.

Tell me about it
When was the last time you just wanted to give up? What did you do?

Think about it
How can hope give us new strength?

DO IT!
Memorize the words of Isaiah 40:31: "Those who trust in the Lord will renew their strength."

A Future and a Hope

"For I know the plans I have for you"—this is the Lord's declaration—"plans for your welfare, not for disaster, to give you a future and a hope."

—Jeremiah 29:11

Just as God spoke the earth into being . . . just as He told the sun to shine . . . just as He declared the light "day" and the darkness "night". . . He has declared His plans for you.

It's hard to imagine, but before we were even born, God had plans for us. "We are His creation, created in Christ Jesus for good works, which God prepared ahead of time so that we should walk in them" (Ephesians 2:10). But to know what those plans are, we need to get to know God Himself. And as we grow closer to Him, we learn more about those plans He has for us.

Walk with Him, and He will lead you right to the plans He has for you.

 **Tell me about it**

What do you want to be when you grow up?

💡 **Think about it**

How could God use that for His plans and purposes?

✋ **DO IT!**

Draw a picture of a grown-up you. Where will you be? What will you be doing?

No matter what you do, how old you get, how far you roam, God will always love you. His love is so big, so never-ending, that we as humans can't even imagine it.

In fact, 1 John 4:8 tells us that "God is love." So, as long as there is God—forever and ever!—there is love.

He loves you so much that "He gave His One and Only Son, so that everyone who believes in Him will not perish but have eternal life" (John 3:16). That, you can be sure, is a love like no other. And that, little one, is a love you can put your hope in.

📣 Tell me about it
How much do you love your pet, your sister, or your parents?

💡 Think about it
Now, just try to imagine how much God loves you.

✋ DO IT!
Draw a big heart, and write the words of John 3:16 in the center.

Get Rid of the Worries

Give all your worries to him, because he cares about you.

—1 Peter 5:7 NCV

Do you know what the opposite of hope is? You guessed it: worry!

Hope is expecting something good to happen. Worry is thinking something bad will happen.

But the Bible tells us, "Don't worry about anything, but in everything, through prayer and petition with thanksgiving, let your requests be made known to God" (Philippians 4:6). I'll admit, that's a lot easier to read than to do. Still, with some practice, you can learn to skip all of the worrying and take it straight to God.

Hope can't grow the way it's supposed to when it's full of worry weeds. So the next time you feel your hope fading, make sure your worry isn't getting in the way. And if it is, well, get it out of there, and give it to God. He will take it from there.

📢 Tell me about it
What are some hopes and some worries you have right now?

💡 Think about it
How does it help to take our worries to God?

✋ DO IT!
Plant a seed, water it, and watch it grow. If any weeds pop up, toss them out immediately!

For thousands of years, the name of Jesus has brought hope to the world. The prophet Isaiah predicted it before Jesus was even born. And in Matthew 12:21, Jesus Himself points back to those words.

When Jesus spoke the words of Matthew 12:21, huge crowds were following Him. They had heard His teachings. They had seen His miracles. And they had put their hope in Him.

After Jesus went back to heaven, His followers continued His teachings. They told of His miracles and His love. They brought sinners to their Savior. And they placed their hope in Him.

Isaiah had predicted it. Jesus was seeing it happen then. And it is still happening today.

The One you put your hope in is a powerful Savior. He is everlasting. He has brought hope to the nations. And He will bring hope to you.

 **Tell me about it**

Talk to a parent or a teacher about a time when our nation has come together and put its hope in the Lord.

💡 **Think about it**

How does it help us as a nation when we put our hope in God?

 **DO IT!**

Find a token of our nation's hope in God.
(Hint: look at that penny in your piggy bank.)

Hope Grows

"But I will hope continually and will praise You more and more.

—Psalm 71:14

Wow! We have looked at *hope* in so many different ways. We've talked about how to find it and keep it. We've talked about the strength it can give us. We've talked about the *opposites* of hope: worry and hopelessness. And we've talked about how hope has shaped the lives of billions of people for thousands of years.

I *hope* by now this little word has become very real and very powerful for you. It's not just a word to be thrown around, as in, "I hope we have ice cream today." It's a powerful tool you can use. It is a force that will grow inside of you and brighten your days—if you will let it.

Keep thinking about it. Keep growing it. Keep *planting* it. You'll be amazed at how high hope grows.

📣 Tell me about it
How has the idea of hope grown for you?

💡 Think about it
What are some ways you can plant hope in the lives of others?

✋ DO IT!
Find one way, today, to plant hope in someone's life.

After all that we've learned about hope, there's one thing that you must never, ever forget: *always hope*.

Those two words will get you through so much. When things seem their darkest. . . when there seems like no way out . . . when you're ready to give up . . . always hope.

It will lift you through the valleys. It will carry you over the mountains. It will give you light when there is none to be found.

The Bible tells us that faith, hope, and love are the three things that will last forever (1 Corinthians 13:13). Whatever may come your way, it will not outlast hope or faith or love.

Hope always. "And always put your hope in God."

 Tell me about it

When you're facing tough times in the future, describe what it will look like to "always put your hope in God."

Think about it

If you know that hope lasts forever, does this change the way you look at your future? How?

DO IT!

Make a sign for your room with the words of Hosea 12:6: "Always put your hope in God."

Walking Together Press is a non-profit publishing company devoted to supporting grassroots libraries in Africa through global book sales and through providing free library editions. To read our story, to see our catalog, and to learn more about how you can help us in our mission, visit our website at:

walkingtogether.press

www.ingramcontent.com/pod-product-compliance
Lightning Source LLC
Chambersburg PA
CBHW042027050526
44107CB00103B/723